THE
Moment
AFTER

JAMES FREEMAN

Copyright © 2023 James Freeman.

All rights reserved. No part of this book may be reproduced, stored, or transmitted by any means—whether auditory, graphic, mechanical, or electronic—without written permission of both publisher and author, except in the case of brief excerpts used in critical articles and reviews. Unauthorized reproduction of any part of this work is illegal and is punishable by law.

ISBN: 979-8-89031-573-1 (sc)
ISBN: 979-8-89031-574-8 (hc)
ISBN: 979-8-89031-575-5 (e)

Because of the dynamic nature of the Internet, any web addresses or links contained in this book may have changed since publication and may no longer be valid. The views expressed in this work are solely those of the author and do not necessarily reflect the views of the publisher, and the publisher hereby disclaims any responsibility for them.

One Galleria Blvd., Suite 1900, Metairie, LA 70001
(504) 702-6708

LETTER OF INTENT

This letter will allow us to be able to look down the corridor of life. To see the end result of a wrong choice of direction, where the ability to change is no longer available, while still standing in a time where change can be made.

To recall moments in life, where decisions were made, to later find that it took us down a road that led to worse times. The difference between those times and the point in this letter is; as long as we are living, the decisions we make, whether bad or good, we can set our mind, buckle down for the ride, and ride it out because better days will come. Many other things can be worked out, gotten over, or pressed through as long as we live. The point of this letter is stressing the fact that there is no chance of change after we die. The course which we choose is set then.

Long before man had trouble, even before he knew trouble; it was first on the scene in the heavens. There was a point before time as we know it, that the angel; head of praise, son of the morning, O Lucifer, conceived and said in his heart, "I will ascend into heaven, I will exalt my throne above the stars of God: I will sit also upon the mount of the congregation, in the side of the north: I will ascend above the heights of the clouds; I will be like the Most High." But rather, it is said of him, I beheld Satan as lightning fall from heaven. How art thou fallen from heaven, yet thou shall be brought down to hell, to the side of the pit. Now his place is about the earth until the Day of Judgment.

Lucifer had moved up in ranks as one of the highest angelic positions in heaven. He was the Head of Praise. He knew how to make the praise pleasing in the sight of God. He was at the top of his perfect ability, at the top of his game, and he did it well. So high that he began to brake down; and the brake down seem to be in his ability to continue to give this kind of praise. He began to recognize the praise as something that he desired for himself. With such heights, he began to form thoughts of self-awareness. He began to form a desire to taking the praise of God for himself. And these thoughts, he wasn't able to think through, nor was he able to hide them, but God knew, and immediately cast it out.

On Lucifer's way down, he - with the thought of his deception, and lies—brought a third of the angels from heaven with him. Now that is powerful influence in the wrong direction.

These angels knew perfection; they knew the perfect presence of God.

This brings out the knowledge that there is someone greater than perfection, and that is God; the God of the universe; the God of all past, present, and future. He is the Most High.

Now from time's beginning, just as Satan deceived the angels, he works that same lie of deception on man, here on earth. All Thanks are to God (Ephesians 1: 4 -6) Lets us know that a way was made for us before the foundation of the world. There was one law for man: (Genesis 2:16)

All that was in the garden was good for man, but there was a commandment given to the man. Of the fruit of the tree that was in the middle of it, he was forbidden to eat.

Satan deceived man, into eating of the forbidden tree that was in the midst of the Garden. He used the serpent, for it was subtler than any beast of the field. He doesn't use a straightforward approach; he comes in a way where you wouldn't recognize.

That satanic influence to man, against God has waxed worse and worse. The influence of self-awareness, and making one's own self gain, is taking shape. One receives power, praise and worth of self as though he was the originator. The deception is that you can be your own self, a–god.

In the day of the first two sons Cain and Abel, evil progressed. When one gift wasn't good enough, instead of making it better, he gets rid of the one with the better gift.

It was said of Satan, is this man that made the earth to tremble, that did shake kingdoms. That made the world as a wilderness, and destroyed the cities thereof. This evil was unleashed.

Though the God of the universe has provided every door to salvation, evil is yet prominent for a season. In man's shame, it is as though he hides from the righteousness of God.

The more he hides, the more comfortable he becomes in darkness. This darkness has embraced the heart of men with boldness. As men, are overtaken by this dark evil grip - allowing its ugly head to rise up without boundaries. The biddings of evil are like a dark cloud settling over the nation. Man wonders around, lost and void of direction. That cloud had gotten so dark, he can't find his way. God sees the state that man is in, but instead of making man turn to His righteousness, He set the plan that gives every man a choice. He set up a light - a pathway back to Him, so that every man has to make the choice of coming back to Him, in the light, or to stay in darkness.

God sent a message to the people back in Noah's day. And the Lord said, "My spirit shall not always strive with man." (Gen. 6:3a.) God say that the wickedness of man was great in the earth, and that every imagination of the thoughts of the heart was evil continually (Gen. 6:5).

The earth also was corrupt before God, and the earth was filled with violence.

God looked upon the earth, and behold, it was corrupt (Gen. 6:11-12a). And God said unto Noah, "The end of all flesh is come before Me; for the earth is fill with violence through them; and behold I will destroy them with the earth. Make thee an Ark of gopher wood (Gen. 6:13,14a). And behold, I, even I, do bring a flood of waters upon the earth, to destroy all flesh (6: 17a). And I will cause it to rain upon the earth forty days and forty nights. (Gen. 7:4a)." Noah preached that same message for a hundred and twenty years, but the people wouldn't hear him.

They laughed at him, for it hadn't rained since the world began, and why would he build an ark on dry land. The people waited until all that would be saved, got in the ark and the door was shut, and the rain started. At that moment, it was too late. This was a type and shadow of that is to come. What choices are we making?

After the flood, God made a promise that He wouldn't destroy the earth with water ever again. He placed a sign in the sky that would remind man of that promise. He said. "It won't be water, but fire next time."

God commissioned man to replenish the earth, though the influence of evil is far from removed.

All in the fullness of time, God provided man with more knowledge of the way back to the path of light. He provided the Law of Commandments in the day of Moses - the awareness of guidelines, and the knowledge of animal sacrifices, as a covering of sins. All of these things were only a prerequisite of True way back to right standings in God.

God raised up prophets from generation to generation, giving them words of things to look and prepare for. God set a plan to send His only son to die as a sacrifice in mans place.

The only True sacrifice that would satisfy the penalty that God set for sin. (Ezekiel 18: 20a). "The soul that sinneth, shall die."

Without God's plan, Satan and his deceit keeps man in darkness and away from God. In many ways, Satan displayed the death of the Son of God, as a victory in his favor. Satan thought, that if he killed the Son, that it would spoil the plan of God. Once again, his thoughts of himself, as being at the top of his game - only to find out, that he couldn't think it through to the capacity of the One and only, Mind of God. Satan's thoughts were evil intended, but God turned it for good. Satan thought that, as he set the fate of the 1st man Adam, he would do also to the 2nd God sent Son. (John 10:17 - 18) Therefore doth My Father love Me, because I lay down My life, that I might take it again. No man taketh it from Me, but I lay it down of Myself.

Now the way is complete. Jesus, the Son of God, was sent to show man the way. He is the Plan of Salvation. He came to pay the penalty for man, for what man could not do, and through His Death, Burial, and Resurrection, it is sealed. God fixed it, and the way is forever established, all man has to do is believe and receive the work of Salvation. In this wonderful plan of Salvation, God through His Son Jesus Christ left us instructions to carry out. (Matthew 28: 19 -20) "Go ye therefore, and teach all nations, baptizing them in the Name of the Father, and of the Son, and of the Holy Ghost: Teaching them to observe all things whatever I have commanded you: and, Lo, I am with you always, even unto the end of the world. Amen." This is what every man needs to change his course from the direction of darkness that leads to an eternal death.

Satan - the deceiver, doesn't give up.

He comes in again with his subtle way of putting a little twist on what man should consider in his belief. He cunningly presses his was into the Church Building and way in any way he can. When he sees one being elevated, he introduces pride, and then subtly feeds it. He targets the emotions to deter the weak.

He puts just enough on it to keep man off the righteous path of God. Satan pulls the wool over the eyes of man, causing him to see a false path; and many will stay in darkness. Satan's endeavor is to keep man's focus on the lust of the flesh, the lust of the eye, and the pride of life.

The grip of darkness holds, though tomorrow isn't promised. His motive is to steal, kill and destroy. His flattery is to cause one to miss-manage the time that he has - for what is not promised.

When one is in darkness, instead of turning to the provided light, he is swayed to wait until tomorrow.

There's a day that has been a long time coming that will be in that same like manner of Noah's day. There will be people standing around and yet being deceived, not taking heed to the warnings. Instead, they make light of the fact that many preachers has come and gone, preaching this message through the ages. The word is being preached in many places on every corner. Technology has enabled the word to go out over the airwaves, on the radio, television, and the Internet. Many still don't see the need to make a change. Don't let it be you!

The curiosity to tamper with chants that defy the God-given goodness that's provided. Such defiance has lead men to think that the lie of evil could indeed over throw good and, therewith, move Satan's seat above God in power.

Satan has the same lie that he told Jesus, after He was baptized. He offers false hope; he offers a kingdom if the worship was given to him.

Satan is still trying to move his seat to be like the light of God, and hides the Truth with a cloud of darkness.

That darkness has taken root and spread out in many directions to further hold man in bondage.

This bondage is masked with a picture to be desired; set before the eyes, and holding the man that will not take heed of the way that God has made. It searches the mind and enhances the desires of the flesh, causing man to crave the unhealthy way. Every generation unleashes greater holds on man. More and more the evil imagination becomes the next step in reality. Then the reality takes on boldness, and a coming out of the closet way of thinking is born. Whether it was a time of one's self, or doing one's own thing, this progression of evil has brought the corruption to as many as would receive it.

Man sees evil as it is, and rationalizes reasons to embrace its viewpoint. Now strength is added in numbers. As the crowd grows, it comforts the mind to except it as being Okay. Beloved, know that the Word of God is True. (Romans 3: 4) God forbid: yea let God be true, but every man a liar.

Darkness and deceit is all in the plan of Satan. He knows that the Lord is coming back one day, but his mind set is bent on moving his seat above the thrown of God. He was defeated and thrown out of the presences of God, when his thoughts first became corrupt. He failed when he under estimated the purpose of the death of Jesus, the Son of God. Satan hasn't given up, so he continues to build his army of the fallen angels, and as many men as would believe the lie that he tells. He is sending men on paths full of false hopes. Evil is at a rampage to gather strength to win a war ahead.

Satan knows that his time is running out, but he is fixed on the thought of spoiling the plan of God, therewith, escaping the sentence set on his head.

This persuasive force is corrupting hearts and minds from every generation.

The God of the Universe is faithful. The Plan of Salvation is to lead the obedient man back to the Presents of God, where life Truly is. Even the corruption, God shines His Light through the believer, and as light comes into the presence of darkness, others can see their way back to the path of Righteousness.

Evil becomes much more fluent in power as men except it as the run-of -the-day thing to do. Now man has, and do hear of the right way, but because man has grown to love darkness rather than light, he takes an active part in the assurance, that others know to do whatever they feel. In so doing, comes the stamp of approval on every evil thing that is brought to the table.

This direction is; make your own definition of what is right.

God has given His Spiritual insight to the believer. If I may give three words to bring some light to us-ward: Perceive, Receive and Deceive.

1) Perceive - before hand.

   God is - Omniscient wise - All Knowing

   - Omni-present - Everywhere at All times.
   - Omni-potent - All Powerful - The Source of.

   So before the Foundation of the World, God made a Way for the believer.

   When the Word came (Lord Jesus) the Scripture shows during His teaching, that He (Jesus) Perceived their thoughts

2) Receive - To humbly except a gift. Jesus told us, the believer to "receive ye the Holy Spirit".

   - The Holy Spirit will lead you into

   All Truth. This gives the believer, which is lower than the Angels (even Satan), but to the believer to receive the Holy Spirit, gives us access over the power of Satan.

3) Deceive - Cause someone to believe something that is not true. Satan is the deceiver. Though Satan can't create anything, he uses deception that you believe his lies rather than the truth.

God is teaching the believer by faith, which is more powerful than that we see. What we see is the result of faith in God. The true Power is in the Word of God. He Spoke the World into existence. Therefore the Power of the Word is greater than the strength of the hand; that which is tangible.

Sex, drugs, and alcohol, are all good in its right context, but the grip of evil has perverted it into something unhealthy, wrong, and not right.

Sex is God-given, and is to be carried out in the boundaries of marriage. And the Lord God said, "It is not good that man should be alone; I will make him a helpmeet for him (Genesis 2:18). Therefore shall a man leave his father and his mother, and shall cleave unto his wife; and they shall be one flesh (Genesis 2:24). Whosoever finds a wife finds a good thing, and obtains favor of the Lord (Proverbs 18:22). Nevertheless, to avoid fornication, let every man have is own wife, and let every woman have her own husband. Let the husband render unto the wife due benevolence: and likewise also the wife unto the husband. The wife hath not power of her own body, but the husband; and likewise also the husband hath not power of his own body, but the wife (1 Corinth. 7:2-4).

Satan has taken that good thing of God and added his lie to it, causing man to error. The lie has caused the good thing to become so corrupt. It has gone from being Okay to marry more than one, to have sex outside of marriage, to having sex with two of the same sex; male with male, or female with female. Now the latest of the corruption is to bring same sex partners into a legal marriage. And as it being is being made legal, therewith, making it illegal to speak against it. To the believer, as Apostle Peter and the other Apostles said in (Acts 5:29) "We must obey God rather than man".

Drugs are good in the boundaries of medicine. God gave man knowledge to use the materials that He provided in the earth to heal the body. The love of God shines through the dark cloud of evil. For the man that has no faith, God gave the physicians. The sinful man was sentenced to death, and that eternally, but God's Love shines through His Grace upon all men, giving all a chance to see the Light and run to safety.

Moderations of alcohol can ease pain and make the heart marry. The first miracle that Jesus performed was at Cana in Galilee. He and the disciples were invited to a marriage. Jesus was informed of His mother that there was no wine. Jesus instructed the servants to fill the water pots with water, and told them to give it to the host of the feast. The host did not know what was to be done. The host said of the wine, "Usually the best is brought out last, after the guess are all full of the lesser wine, but here the best is brought out last" (John 2: 1-11). And be not drunk with wine, wherein is excess; but be filled with the Spirit (Ephesians 5:18). Satan brought his lies and led man to believe that there are no limits. Man becomes more comfortable in darkness.

> *Satan didn't tell man that when he is in this state of no limits that he always go farther than he expected to go and stay longer than he expected to stay. Therefore, it will be harder to see the way out that he expected to see.*

Though man knows the direction of this evil and that its end has been fore told through the preached Word of God. "Behold, all souls are mine; as the soul of the father, so also the soul of the son is mine: the soul that continue in sin, it shall die" (Ezekiel 18:4). For the wages of sin is death; but the gift of God is eternal life through Jesus Christ our Lord (Romans 6:23).

The negative influence portrays, that the God of righteousness has gone to sleep, and all things continue as they were from the beginning of the creation. The Lord is not slack concerning his promise, as some men count slackness; but longsuffering to us-ward, not willing that any should perish, but that all should come to repentance. But the day of the Lord will come as a thief in the night; (2 Peter 3:4, 9-10a). "Behold, I come quickly: blessed is he that keeps the sayings of the prophecy of the book" (Revelation 22: 7). And, "Behold, I come quickly; and my reward is with me, to give every man according as his work shall be.

I am Alpha and Omega, the beginning and the end, the first and the last" (Revelation 22: 12-13). At that time, the decisions that are made, will be the decisions set for judgment. He that is unjust, let him be unjust still: and he who is filthy, let him be filthy still: and he that is righteous, let him be righteous still: and he that is holy, let him be holy still (Revelation 22: 11).

The fool has said in his heart, "There is no God" (Psalm 14:1a). Mesmerized like a drug that hides the worries and cares, the heart of that man is transfixed on the lie from Satan. One brought into deception and buys it, void of rational thinking. He is a fish being pulled out of water - receiving it all: hook, line and sinker. It's part of the bait of Satan's trap of deception. The trap is loaded with many goodies to lour one into the snare. Satan is not your friend. He is still out to steal, kill and destroy.

Like a train headed down the track, and no one takes heed of the awareness that the bridge is out ahead. The trine of the day is, anything goes, so eat, drink, and be merry; we will die some how.

Let it be said. "All that are on this train - get off." Receive and believe the Plan of Salvation.

The Lord Jesus put His life on the line that whosoever will, shall be Saved. (Matthew 14: 30b -31) Peter beginning to sink, he cried, saying, "Lord Save me." And immediately Jesus stretched forth His hand, and caught him. Don't stay because of the crowd. The cry is made. This train leads to destruction.

A PICTURE STORYLINE

Artwork by
JAMES FREEMAN

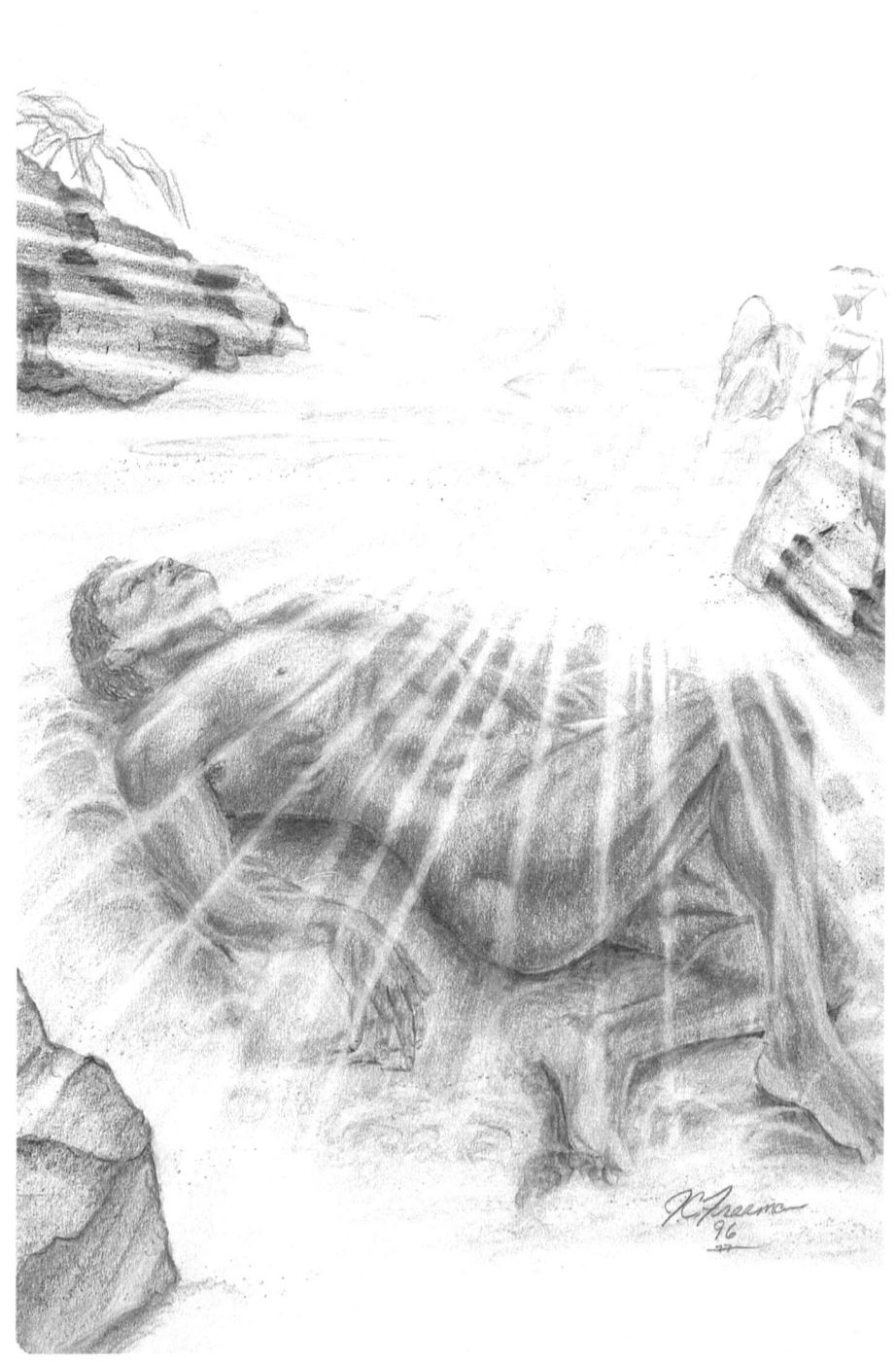

In the beginning God created the Heaven and the earth, and the fullness thereof. Then He spoke and said; it was good. Then Satan came in with his lie and corrupted it.

Joseph ran from Potiphar's wife, when she made an advance on him. His integrity caused him to be cast into prison, but God was with him. God raised him up, and was next in power to the pharaoh.

God told Moses to lead the chosen people out of the land of Egypt.
God showed Moses and the people that there is no obstacle that can stand in His way.

Samson was one of the judges that God raised up. God put His strength in the man, and his hair was not to be cut. Satan brought in cunning distractions to bring the man down, but in his ending; he called on God, and God stepped in and justified.

Daniel prayed to God three times a day. Satan, through the king, put out a decree that all will worship the god that he had set up. Daniel did not comply and was thrown in a lions den. God closed the mouths of the lions, and Daniel slept with them all night.

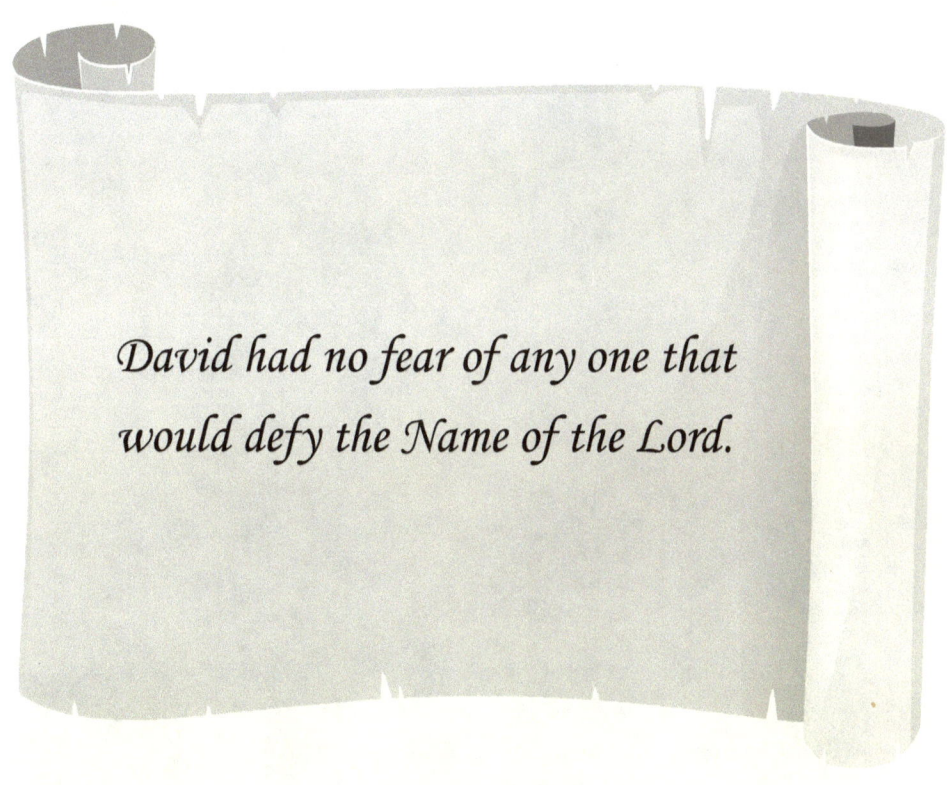

David had no fear of any one that would defy the Name of the Lord.

Jonah was a man of God that allowed Satan to distort his view of the goodness of God. He was told of God, to go preach to the Ninevites. Jonah complained and ran the other way; to Tarshish instead. God brought him back in the belly of a big fish.

Mary was used to bring forth the Son of God in Bethlehem. Satan tried to have Him killed, but God told Joseph in a dream, to go to Egypt.

The Son of God; He is the Sacrifice for the sins of the world. Whosoever would believe on Him, shall be saved.

The borrowed tomb of the resurrected Jesus was sealed with a great stone and two soldiers guarded it. When the Lord was ready to move, the soldiers was put in a deep sleep and the stone moved.

Saul thought he was working for God by stamping out the one's that would follow Jesus; the Christ. This was another deception of Satan. Jesus divinely showed up on Saul's journey to Damascus.

Now the mark of the beast isn't just one man, but unbelief - the very rejection of God's righteousness. A very devastating choice made in the wrong direction; but it's only a ploy to false hope, and leading men to believe a lie. A choice like this is like a man that builds his house on sand. The initial; subtle influence to look over his foundation situation, isn't far from his mind at the beginning. He continues to build, ignoring the truth that is being further covered.

He builds the floor; he builds the walls;
by the time he gets to the roof,
those thoughts of the weak foundation are small.

At every stage, he knew he should take control,
but the bad influence says, "go for it, the weight will hold."

So he builds and builds until the house has taken form.
The thought of the foundation is out of sight and out of mind
until the storm.

The storm came with winds and rain;
And after all the work, time and labor is destroyed;
Nothing remained.

The warning remains, through the teach word, and the preach word, that the Lord sends to anyone who will hear and seek out the righteous path that is set up. "Watch therefore: for ye know not what hour your Lord doth come".

Good is rejected from every facet to further pull the wool over the eyes of men and keep men in darkness and, therefore, believing a lie. Prayer was being taken out of schools. A judgment was raised to take the Ten Commandments out of courtrooms. The move was inn to take, "In God We Trust" off the money. On and on, evil is perverted and twisted, and many are following like a landslide.

This road that evil has many traveling on seems easy and fulfilling, but the reality must kick in. The truth is out to change the course. We must reach for it before the there is no time left. Make God the choice; He will help us see.

The Plan of Salvation is in place. We must see the signs. God made man in his image. Man fell into sin by the trick of Satan. The wages of sin is death, but God, through the Grace His Son Jesus Christ; the Death, Burial and Resurrection, the way is made for the believer. All of these things are in place already. God left a part for the Church to do after Jesus left. The disciples were the starters of the Church and Jesus breathed on them, saying, "Receive the Holy Spirit" (John 20:22). Jesus said, "But ye shall receive power, after that the Holy Ghost is come upon you: and you shall be witnesses unto Me both in Jerusalem, and in all Judaea, and in Samaria, and unto the uttermost part of the earth" (Acts 1: 8). He said, "Go ye into all the world, and preach the Gospel to every creature. He that believeth and is baptized shall be saved" (Mark 16: 15-16). The Lord is not slack concerning His promise, as some men count slackness; but is longsuffering to us-ward, not willing that any should perish, but that all should come to repentance. But the day of the Lord will come as a thief in the night; (2 Peter 3:9-10). The Church is to Preach the Gospel, that He reach, each individual, making available the opportunity for renewed life. Though the Word is being carried over the airwaves through radio, Internet medias, the Church still should view that as the work of one. The Love of God constrains us, not to view any opportunity as someone else is taking care of that one. Every believer must keep his Light of Christ on at all times to give freely anywhere darkness may appear.

The enemy is working hard at keeping the blinders over the eyes of the lost.

They are not listening to Christian Media as a norm. The Church must make and keep it personal to seize every chance for Salvation. We work while it is day, for when night comes, no man can work.

The Day Will Come

Then the day came; that dreadful hour appeared. The moment of truth has come. In a twinkling of an eye; the trumpet sound. The corruptible must put on incorruption, and the mortal must put on immortality (1 Corinthians 15:52,53).

Then shall two be in the field; the one shall be taken, and the other left. Two women shall be grinding at the mill; the one shall be taken, and the other left (Matthew 24:40,41).

Then when the moment has passed;
That state that he is in, holds fast.

It all becomes real in the eyes of those who were deceived.
My fate is set now; I should have believed.

Oh, how the time that uses to seem to stand still, has come and gone.
All in a Moment, that influential boldness,
changed to fear, down to the bone.

The awareness of the long-time statement,
"Don't let it be said too late."
It has come up for questioning in the mind.
"How did I miscalculate?

How could this, not be foreseen?
This state, which I'm now in. "What does it mean?

How did I not take any precautions?
Woe am I, in my state of exhaustion.

This short-lived pleasure has caused me to be left behind.
I can't blame anyone; the fault is all mine.

Whereas of now, I know not what tomorrow holds.
I will make the Good Choice, and set some goals.

Whereas ye know not what shall be on the morrow. For what is your life? It is even a vapor that appears for a little time, and then vanished away (James 4:14).

It was in this vapor space called life that every man, woman, boy, and girl has to make the choice to follow good or evil. Within that time, God set before man good and evil, and through His word, He said, "Choose ye this day whom ye will serve." After this life, the moment after, there is no choice.

Then evil disguised itself, with man's instinct to survive, to gain control of the minds- again, with one accord. "You can be your own selves- gods. You have been to the heavens and you have ruled this world. You can also escape the sentence that was placed on your head. Just because you didn't choose His way, there is another way. With all the skill and knowledge man has, you must just find a weakness.

With your weapons of warfare, you can call down fire from the heavens. How many wonders have you already discovered, and as you set your mind to it, you will do more."

After being deceived once again, the evil persuades man to get ready to do battle with the Lord. And Satan will lead them. So the thought was conceived. "We will become self-sufficient."

To no avail, and all in a moment, like lightening, the thought came to naught.

And I saw an angel come down from heaven, having the key of the bottomless pit and a great chain in his hand. And he laid hold on the dragon, that old serpent, which is the Devil, and Satan, and bound him a thousand years. And cast him into the bottomless pit, and shut him up, and set a seal upon him, that he should deceive the nation no more, till the thousand years should be fulfilled (Rev. 20:1-3).

This was another phase of deception uncovered- now realizing they were in a too late state for the heart could only be changed through salvation, which is no longer available.

And the fifth angel sounded, and I saw a star fall from heaven unto the earth: and to him was given the key to the bottomless pit. And he opens the bottomless pit; and there arose a smoke out of the pit, as the smoke of a great furnace; and the sun and the air were darkened by reason of the smoke of the pit.

And there came out of the smoke, locusts upon the earth: and to them was given power, as the scorpions of the earth have power. And it was commanded them that they should not hurt the grass of the earth, neither any green thing, neither any trees; but only those men which have not the seal of God in their foreheads (Rev.9: 1-4).

The sting of the locusts wasn't to kill man, but it should torment them for five months. And in those days shall men seek death, and shall not find it; and shall desire to die; death shall flee from them (Rev.9: 5, 6).

There are no more clouds to cover the truth. The choice that was made can be clearly seen that it was the wrong one, and man realize it can't be changed. The judgment is set. In their search, they cry for the rocks to fall on them. They turned their own weapons on themselves to no avail. Their blood is spilled in the streets until it was up to the horse's bib. They wished for death, but it was not to be found.

Now all that happens after that moment- the moment of separation, the moment that truth is revealed and that deception curtain is pulled back and the ability to accept change is out of reach.

This thought, is to open up the "view port of time"- to show a route in which not to take.

Don't be deceived; there's a better way. The God of all creation has made a plan of salvation, which is through His son Jesus Christ.

Now! This is the time before the moment; that change must be made. This is the word we preach.

Make The Change

That if you shall confess with your mouth the Lord Jesus, and shall believe in your heart that God has raised him from the dead, you shall be saved (Romans 10:9).

DO IT NOW...
BEFORE THE
MOMENT...

Repeat this prayer openly from the heart.

Lord Jesus; I repent of all my sins, forgive me; for I believe that God the Father sent you to show us the way, and in that, You suffered and died on the cross, as a sacrifice for our sins, and was buried. On the third day God the Father raised you from the dead. Now Lord Jesus; I receive you into my heart as my Lord and savior.

RECORDING

MY NEW BIRTH IN CHRIST JESUS

Date: _____

Testimony: _____

_____
_____
_____
_____
_____
_____
_____
_____
_____
_____
_____
_____
_____
_____
_____
_____
_____
_____
_____
_____
_____
_____
_____
_____
_____
_____

Now that you've accepted Christ Jesus as your Lord and Savior; get into a Bible based Church so you can grow. Here are a few tips in scripture, to help you get started.

But ye shall receive power, after that the Holy Ghost is come upon you: ye shall be witnesses unto me both in Jerusalem, and in all Ju-dae'a, and in Samaria, and unto the uttermost part of the earth (Acts 1:8).

As newborn babes, desire the sincere milk of the word that ye may grow thereby (1 Peter 2:2)

Take my yoke upon you, and learn of me; for I am meek and lowly in heart: and ye shall find rest unto your souls. For my yoke is easy, and my burden is light (Matthew 11:29,30).

For whosoever shall call upon the name of the Lord shall be saved. How then shall they call on him in whom they have not believed?

And how shall they believe in him of whom they have not heard? And how shall they hear without a preacher? And how shall they preach except they be sent? (Romans 10:13-15a)

Study to show thyself approved unto God, a workman that need not to be ashamed, rightly dividing the word of truth (2 Timothy 2:15).

Trust in the Lord with all thine heart; and lean not unto your own understanding. In all thy ways acknowledge him, and he shall direct thy paths (Proverbs 3:5,6).

Then said Jesus to those Jews which believed on him, if ye continue in my word, then are ye my disciples indeed; and ye shall know the truth, and the truth shall make you free (St. John 8:31,32).

JAMES FREEMAN
artlines64@yahoo.com

"I am but a servant, but a soldier in the Army of the Lord. I know that to be meek is to have strength under control. I am humbled and realize that it is such a privilege to even handle the precious Word of God. I am reminded of the two Commandments that the Lord Jesus gave us; 'Love the Lord God with all of our heart; and to Love our neighbor as ourselves.' Therefore, with the same awareness I have for myself, I made others aware also. Two portions of scriptures that are often put together come to mind; (Ecclesiastes 9: 11b and Matthew 10: 22b) "The race is not to the swift or the battle to the strong, but he who endures to the end shall be saved."

I have found that God has a wonderful plan for all who receive Him as Lord and Savior.

Now I humbly ask you to take a serious look at the direction of your life and let the Bible be your guide.

"MAKE A CHOICE WHILE
CHANGE CAN BE MADE."

www.ingramcontent.com/pod-product-compliance
Lightning Source LLC
LaVergne TN
LVHW041636070526
838199LV00052B/3398